# The Life God Intended

*Living Naturally Supernatural*

**GARY OATES**

***with***

**Robert Paul Lamb**

**Open Heaven Publications**

*an outreach of Gary Oates Ministries, Inc.*

P.O. Box 457/Moravian Falls, NC 28654

336-667-2333

**The Life God Intended**



ISBN 978-0-9752622-3-8

Requests for information should be directed to:

**Open Heaven Publications**
P.O. Box 457/Moravian Falls, NC 28654
336-667-2333



Printed in the United States of America

*"For physical training is of some value (useful for a little), but godliness (spiritual training) is useful and of value in everything and in every way, for it holds promise for the present life and also for the life which is to come."*

1 Timothy 4:8
Amplified Bible

# Table of Contents

# Introduction

Did you know that God has a divine purpose and destiny for your life and for every living person on this "blue marble" of a planet?

The apostle Paul explains the Lord's divine intention for each of us with these words: *"...Who has saved us and called us to a holy life—not because of anything we have done but because of His own purpose and grace... given us in Christ Jesus before the beginning of time,"* (1 Timothy 1:9 NIV).

That "holy life" involves living the life God intended. It literally means embracing His purpose and destiny for our lives, the Gifts of the Spirit, the Fruit of the Spirit, and walking in the supernatural dimension while we are upon the Earth.

I am convinced that living anything less is clearly not the life God intended for His people.

On his television program, my friend Sid Roth frequently challenges his viewers with the bold exhortation that all followers of Jesus should "become *naturally* supernatural!"

Of course, many of God's people may not know the word "supernatural" does not appear in the Bible. There's no such thing as the supernatural with God. It's all natural with the Creator of heaven and earth, but the concept of the supernatural is well expressed throughout the Scriptures.

It's supernatural with believers because it is beyond our natural capabilities. Yet, each of us should want to have the supernatural operative in our lives since it is representative of the character and nature of Almighty God.

But there is an important question that must be asked for those desiring to become naturally supernatural. Are you willing to pay the price for it?

I have people coming up to me all the time saying, "I want a *double* portion of what you have...pray for me to have it."

My frequent response is: "I'd like to have a double portion also, but I can't honestly give you something I don't have."

Most people appear to want a big experience with God.

I've heard people say such things as "If I can just go into the throne room and have an encounter with God, I know everything is going to change in my life."

Yet, I've witnessed just the opposite happening with the majority of people. They seemingly have an encounter with the Lord and nothing significant ever changes in their lives.

Why? Because each of us must daily "walk out" in practical dimensions the supernatural experiences we have had.

Several years ago I was in Bordertown, Australia, teaching in a School of Ministry with long-time friend, Pastor Bill Johnson. "Are you still seeing angels?" he asked one day.

"Well, actually yes," I answered. "It continues to increase."

"That's unusual," he responded, "because a lot of people have an experience like yours and they ultimately write a book. Before long, they get caught up in the glamour of their experience, lose their anointing and are never heard from again."

As I pondered Bill's words, he asked a second question. "What do you attribute to your continuing experiences?"

"Developing an intimate relationship with the Father is the key," I replied. "I have discovered that I must experience God's manifest presence every day. That's not a 'Sunday only' event in preparation for a time of ministry. It's a daily encounter with the Lord. Without that, no *genuine* ministry can ever truly come forth as God intended."

Of the notable stories in Scripture, Joseph's is one of the most powerful examples that an intimate relationship with God is absolutely essential to discovering the life the Almighty intended. Joseph demonstrated that God-centered life with his conniving brothers, in Potiphar's house and even in his years of being wrongly imprisoned. In God's timing he became the second most powerful man in Egypt.

Genesis 50:20 (NIV) demonstrates the divine perspective Joseph gained from his own life. *"You intended to harm me,"* he said to his brothers, *"<u>but God intended</u> it for good to accomplish what is now being done, the saving of many lives."*

In truth, there is a great price to pay for having supernatural encounters with the living God. Over the years, I've learned that many believers have never grasped that crucial truth.

Some time ago I was having a morning walk in Moravian Falls near my home, and two women pulled up beside me in a car and began talking. After a few minutes chatting, the lady driving asked, "Would you pray for me to lose weight?"

"Sure," I said, "but first, why don't you park the car and walk with me?"

"Oh, no. I don't want to lose weight that way," she answered quickly. "I want God to just take it all off...I don't want to have to change my lifestyle or the way I eat. Exercise and discipline aren't for me. I just want God to do it."

Does anybody honestly think that woman's request will be answered? I hardly think so.

Just like this woman, some in the church have bought into entitlement—that I can have whatever I want no matter the circumstances.

Yet, I can tell you that I have seen people, who had a right attitude with God, lose all kinds of weight *instantly*. Some had dreadful physical problems. Others had made unwise choices in daily living.

But God sovereignly and supernaturally answered their heartfelt petitions. That is always characteristic and true of our heavenly Father, the One who functions in great supernatural manifestations on behalf of His children.

After all, we are *"a kind of firstfruits of all His creatures [a sample of what He created to be consecrated to Himself]."* (James 1:18 Amplified).

Gary Oates
Moravian Falls, NC

## Chapter 1

# Risky Living

*"...If you are needy, if your inner person is lonely, empty, and confused...Happiness is possible...I'm talking about risky living. The kind that, if practiced, will turn your entire world upside down. But, what's the use of living if you don't attempt the impossible..."*

— from *Risky Living* by Jamie Buckingham

After years of travel—planting churches from the ground up in three different states (Washington, Tennessee, Georgia), and pastoring those fledgling congregations—my wife and I moved to the east coast of Florida with our two daughters.

It was there in the late 1980s that I faced total "burn out" from ministry. Outwardly, the picture may have looked good to somebody else. The church was growing, even flourishing in some respects.

But I was exhausted and dying on the inside. I had become empty and miserable in my innermost being, and I *knew* I was just going through the motions of being a pastor. I had to make a change.

Ultimately, I decided to take a six months sabbatical from ministry to reevaluate what I needed to do with my life. That six months actually stretched into 3½ years. To support my family, I took a job as a stockbroker.

Having closed the church, I grew embittered and angry with God. I stopped praying and reading the Bible. It was even painful for me to attend church because I felt such a failure at pastoring. The only reason I even bothered going was because of our small children.

In time, I became very successful as a stockbroker. I couldn't believe the money I was earning. Yet, I was still empty and miserable on the inside. A sense of desperation hung over me.

The enemy of my soul was constantly telling me that I had never been called to the ministry. "You've wasted the best years of your life pursuing a dead end street", he belittled me.

In my office one day, I was reading my new Bible—*The Wall Street Journal*, and I came across an article headlined "The Time to Change Is Before You Have To."

*Instantly*, I knew God was speaking to me. Yet, what was He saying?

Two questions immediately came to mind. Did I want to be a stockbroker for the rest of my life? I knew the answer to that question was "no."

Did I want to go back into the ministry? The answer to that question was *absolutely* not! Never again! I wanted to stay as far away from ministry for the rest of my days.

I was faced with a choice. It was a formidable gamble. Would I risk it all to find the answer to my inner turmoil?

Inwardly, I knew the answer to my own question, and I resigned my job as a stockbroker. I left that successful job with a nationally-known company with absolutely nothing to do in its place.

It was only then that I recognized a faintly lighted candle still burned in my heart to seek God. In that place I desired to know God—*again*.

Thus, I began reading the Bible, praying and seeking the face of God like never before. Soon I felt the Lord was telling me that He *had* called me to the ministry, and that there was a place for me. I had a sense that I needed to go somewhere at His direction and plant another church.

I decided I would not attempt planting another church without *first* speaking to my wife, Kathi. In the meanwhile I would wait and pray.

About three months later, she came to me one day. "You may think I'm crazy," she said with a knowing smile, "but I feel some day we are going to be back in the ministry."

*That* was my confirmation. I knew her words were God's prompting to begin again the process of following His leading. We then began to pursue God in prayer as to where we should go and what we should do.

We decided to move to another city where we planted our fifth congregation. It was in that place that we purposed this church would be open to the leading of the Holy Spirit. He would direct our paths with whatever He wanted to do in this new church.

Never again would I function in self-effort, control or manipulation—all of which I knew had led to my frustration and "burn out". I had to step aside so I could be genuinely led by the Holy Spirit

Of course, it was during that fifth pastorate I began earnestly seeking the Lord, and traveling on mission trips to South America with internationally-known evangelist Randy Clark. Ultimately, I had the experience of being taken up into the presence of the Lord as detailed in the book, *Open My Eyes, Lord.*

Yet, none of the current worldwide ministry that has now touched thousands of lives in North and South America, Europe and other parts of the world would have ever happened without pursuing God in that miracle-birthing dimension of taking great risks.

I discovered that following God is letting go of the old—sometimes breaking tradition—and stepping into the unknown with Him. I once heard the Vineyard's founder, John Wimber say that you spell faith with these letters *r-i-s-k*.

From the very beginning, it seems taking a God-called risk became a major part of living the life God intended for me.

As Jamie Buckingham wisely wrote almost forty years ago in his insightful book: it's truly attempting "the impossible..."

**Chapter 2**

# Walk in the Spirit

*"But I say, walk by the Spirit, and you will not carry out the desire of the flesh."*

— Galatians 5:16 (NASB)

Do you spend much time attempting to overcome the flesh in your life?

I have noticed the Christian marketplace is seemingly filled with books, CD's and DVD's on the subject and yet, many of us are still dealing with the same issues of trying to defeat the flesh in our lives.

The Scripture's admonition (Galatians 5:16 NASB) is

that we *"walk by the Spirit"* and we *"will not carry out the desire of the flesh."*

Consider these two basic questions: What if we practiced exercising our spiritual senses every day instead of griping and complaining to God about the misery and garbage we go through all the time?

And, what if we spent as much time developing our walk in the Spirit as we do trying to overcome the flesh?

Verse 17 says *"For the flesh sets its desire against the Spirit, and the Spirit against the flesh..."* That's the constant battle each of us faces on an unending basis. The problem is that the flesh usually wins the war and the Spirit ends up taking the back seat.

*"...For these are in opposition to one another, so that you may not do the things that you please."* The flesh and the Spirit are total opposites and they are in mortal combat with one another. It seems most of us want to overcome the flesh but we are doing little to develop our spirit.

How can we as believers become *naturally* supernatural without developing our spirit? The sad truth is: we can not!

Galatians 5:18-21 details the terrible "deeds" of the flesh and the benefits as a child of God. *"But if you are led by the Spirit, you are not under the Law.*
*"Now the deeds of the flesh are evident, which are: immorality, impurity, sensuality,*
*"Idolatry, sorcery, enmities, strife, jealousy, outbursts*

*of anger, disputes, dissensions, factions,*

*"Envying, drunkenness, carousing, and things like these, of which I forewarn you, just as I have forewarned you, that those who practice such things will not inherit the kingdom of God."*

So, these are the areas of the flesh that each of us must confront in our lives. It is a difficult struggle as any mature believer would readily admit.

Verses 22-23 continues *"But the fruit of the Spirit is love, joy, peace, patience, kindness, goodness, faithfulness, gentleness, self-control; against such things there is no law."*

Which list sounds better to you—the deeds of the flesh or the fruit of the Spirit? Would you rather live from the fruit of the Spirit (which is supernatural) or the deeds of the flesh (which is doomed to fail)?

Actually, it's a no-brainer as far as decisions go. On the one hand, it's what we all say we want, but we continue battling through fleshly means. Even worse, we are not developing our spirit.

Verses 24-25 tells us *"Now those who belong to Christ Jesus have crucified the flesh with its passions and desires. If we live by the Spirit, let us also <u>walk by the Spirit</u>."*

The Amplified Bible conveys verse 25 in these memorable words: *"...[If by the Holy Spirit we have our life in God, let us go forward walking in line, <u>our conduct controlled by the Spirit</u>.]"*

Notice that the Amplified version emphasizes our conduct will be controlled *"by the Spirit"* not by our impulses, selfish desires or temperament. The word *"controlled"* implies a yieldedness to God in what we say or do, and how we act and what we think.

Truly, our lives in God are then "in-line" with divine purpose and destiny.

## Jesus Points to the Spirit

Jesus makes this astounding statement in John 16:13 (NASB), *"But when He, the Spirit of truth, comes, He will guide you into all the truth..."*

Here is the simple truth (according to Jesus): Learn to walk in the Spirit, be guided by the Spirit and you will not fall prey to the spirit of deception that is so prevalent in the world today.

With the Holy Spirit's guidance, you will be in the right place at the right time. You will even get *that* parking place!

*"...For He will not speak on His own initiative, but whatever He hears, He will speak; and He will disclose to you what is to come."*

The Holy Spirit will solely speak what God is saying—nothing else. He is not going to speak on His own initiative. He is going to say *only* what the Father is saying.

Because the Holy Spirit abides within us, He will guide our very steps—including those pivotal steps that involve our decision-making with our God-called destiny. He will speak in such a way that we can hear His voice.

Importantly, He will *"disclose...what is to come."* That word *"disclose"* contains a significant meaning. Its literal meaning is to show, reveal, manifest.

He will give revelatory understanding of events before they come about and we will understand the Spirit's role in what is being shown. Our spiritual eyes and ears will be opened, and we will be able to respond to His direction for our lives.

## A Promise to Those Who Love Him

If you were asked the simple question: "Do you love Jesus?", how would you answer?

You might say: "That's a pretty dumb question. Of course, I love the Lord."

But listen closely to John 14:15 (NASB) which calls our attention to the words of Jesus regarding those who *"love"* Him. He says, *"If you love Me, you will keep My commandments."*

He repeats similar words about "loving" Him in three additional verses in that same chapter: John 14:21, *"He who has My commandments and keeps them is the one who loves Me..."*; John 14:23, *"...If anyone loves Me, he will keep My word"*; John 14:24, *"He who does not love Me does not keep My word."*

Amazingly, Jesus says the same thing four times in

nine verses. Why would He speak so pointedly to us? Could it be that He wants us to listen very carefully and to walk obediently?

It's obvious (from Jesus' words) that we demonstrate our love to Him by walking in obedience and keeping His commandments. Could there be anything more important in our lives than that?

The Amplified Bible renders verse 21 with this incredible statement: *"...and I [too] will love him and will show [reveal, manifest] Myself to him. [I will let Myself be clearly seen by him and make Myself real to him.]"*

Thus, the person who loves God and is walking in obedience to what God says will step into a phenomenal level of intimacy with Jesus. An intimacy where the Lord of all glory will reveal Himself and show Himself to the obedient.

Proverbs 3:32 (NASB) speaks of the Lord being *"intimate with the upright."* But the Amplified Bible conveys that same passage in such expressive words that stand in overwhelming agreement with what Jesus says in John 14.

*"...His confidential communion and secret counsel are with the [uncompromisingly] righteous (those who are upright and in right standing with Him)."*

The Scriptures speak with a singular voice on this matter: our obedience to God and our love for the Savior draws us into dynamic realms of communion and counsel with Him.

Here is a central question that each believer must legitimately answer before God. Have you genuinely obeyed the last instruction the Lord gave you? It is a basic question that reveals our love for Him.

According to John 14, a believer who truly loves the Lord Jesus will be obedient to God's direction. We must ask ourselves have we obeyed Him?

That's a question I had to ask of a well-to-do woman who made a commitment to Jesus at our church years ago. Unfortunately, it wasn't long before I had a late night phone call from a bar asking Kathi and I to come retrieve this same lady.

She had become discouraged over some personal matter and spent the evening drinking until she was absolutely "loaded". She could hardly walk but we managed to safely get her into our car.

"But-t-t-t...ya know," she slurred as we drove away from the bar, "I real-l-l-y love Je-sus!"

A reasonable person would have to ask: "Really? You really love Jesus? But your drunken conduct contradicts everything you're claiming."

Sadly, it reflects many situations in the Body of Christ where people claim a flawed obedience to Jesus but actually live in disobedience to Him.

## Obedience Is Crucial

Numbers 13 and 14 contains the ancient tale of the

twelve Hebrew spies being sent by Moses into the "promised land" to checkout God's provision. Unfortunately, when they returned from their surveying trip, ten of the spies proclaimed conquering the land was an impossible task.

Numbers 13:32-33 (NASB) tells us *"The land through which we have gone, in spying it out, is a land that devours its inhabitants; and all the people whom we saw in it are men of great size...and we became like grasshoppers in our* own sight, *and so we were in their sight."*

Yet, their conclusion contradicted the very words God had declared about the land. *"I am going to give to the sons of Israel..."* (Numbers 13:1).

Two of the spies—Joshua and Caleb—agreed with God. They saw God as bigger than the giants. In fact, Caleb said *"We should by all means go up and take possession of it, for we will surely overcome it."*

From the story, we learn that those who rebelled against God never entered the "promised land". But those like Joshua and Caleb were rewarded.

In particular, the Lord confirms the difference with Caleb. *"But my servant Caleb, because he has had a different spirit and has <u>followed Me fully</u>, I will bring him into the land which he entered and <u>his descendants shall take possession of it</u>,"* (Numbers 14:24).

Caleb's decision to follow the Lord "fully" is exactly how I want to live my own life. I want to have a *different* spirit.

Of course, that kind of living is always risky. There's always a possibility of hazardous challenges in following God, and even the potential of overwhelming failure. Yet, I want to follow God's direction no matter what anyone else does.

Notice that Caleb's decision was destined to touch the lives of future *"descendants."* When we choose to follow the Spirit of God, that decision will impact our children and our children's children for generations.

Unfortunately, some of us have botched entering our own promised land because we failed to be led by the Spirit of God. Somehow we bought into the spirit of the world and thus, we don't have that *differen*t kind of spirit that will follow God no matter what!

This kind of obedience is crucial to our understanding of becoming naturally supernatural. Don't miss out on believing God for His highest and best for your life. It will lead you to the life He intended.

## Chapter 3

# Spirit, Soul and Body

*"Now may the God of peace Himself sanctify you entirely; and may your spirit and soul and body be preserved complete, without blame at the coming of our Lord Jesus Christ."*

— 1 Thessalonians 5:23 (NASB)

There is a great mystery concerning the true nature of our spirit, soul, and body which comprises the nature of each person upon this planet.

The New King James Version presents 1 Thess. 5:23 with slightly different wording, *"Now may the God of peace Himself sanctify you completely; and may your whole spirit, soul, and body be preserved blameless at the coming of our Lord Jesus Christ."*

Notice the expression *"whole spirit, soul, and body"* in this translation. It is the divine order of the way our Father created us—spirit first, soul second, and then body third. This order also confirms the fact that spiritual laws have higher authority than either mental or physical laws.

The Amplified Bible also presents 1 Thess. 5:23 in an eye-opening manner. *"And may the God of peace Himself sanctify you through and through—that is, separate you from profane things, make you pure and wholly consecrated to God—and may your spirit and soul and body be preserved sound and complete [and found] blameless at the coming of our Lord Jesus Christ, the Messiah."*

Notice that the work of God in a believer's life is intended to be *"through and through..."* and *"separate you from profane things."* God intends that His people will be *"pure and wholly consecrated"* to Him.

Thus, the end result of the Lord's interior work in our three-part being would make us *"sound and complete... and blameless at the coming"* of Jesus.

In addressing the power of God's Word, Hebrews 4:12 (Amplified) connects with this triune nature of mankind. Listen to these awesome words:

*"...It is sharper than any two-edged sword, penetrating to the dividing line of the breath of life (soul) and [the*

*immortal] spirit, and of joints and marrow [that is, of the deepest parts of our nature] exposing and sifting and analyzing and judging the very thoughts and purposes of the heart."*

**God's Indwelling Presence**

When a person is born again or "born from above", the Holy Spirit comes to dwell within that individual's innermost being. Your spirit then begins taking on the nature of God. Romans 8:9 (NASB) confirms that experience in this manner:

*"...You are not in the flesh but in the Spirit, if indeed the Spirit of God dwells in you. But if anyone does not have the Spirit of Christ, he does not belong to Him"*

The word "indwell" means "to exist as an animating or divine inner spirit, force or principle."

The Amplified Bible's version of Romans 8:9 says *"... you are living the life of the Spirit, if the [Holy] Spirit of God [really] dwells within you—directs and controls you. But if anyone does not possess the [Holy] Spirit of Christ, he is none of His [he does not belong to Christ, is not truly a child of God]."*

Galatians 4:6 (NASB) adds this distinctive note about God's work in us. *"Because you are sons, God has sent forth the Spirit of His Son into our hearts, crying 'Abba! Father'!"*

**Spirit, Soul & Body**

In the formative days of my biblical training I was

taught that this triune being of man was best illustrated through three concentric circles. Each facet of our being (spirit, soul and body) operates independently of the other parts.

However, I have come to believe after years of study and observation that the nature of man (illustrated by the three concentric circles) is not the way it actually is. All three are actually interconnected. In a manner of speaking, they all overlap as illustrated below.

If you are under continual great physical attack with an illness, you can also be affected emotionally. By the same token, you can also be impacted spiritually by an attack upon your physical body.

The reverse is also true. If you are battling dangerous stress or strain emotionally, does that affect a person physically? The answer is clearly yes. But I have also learned that such life-threatening stress can have the same affect spiritually as well.

Thus, we realize our spirit, soul and body are truly interconnected by God's divine design.

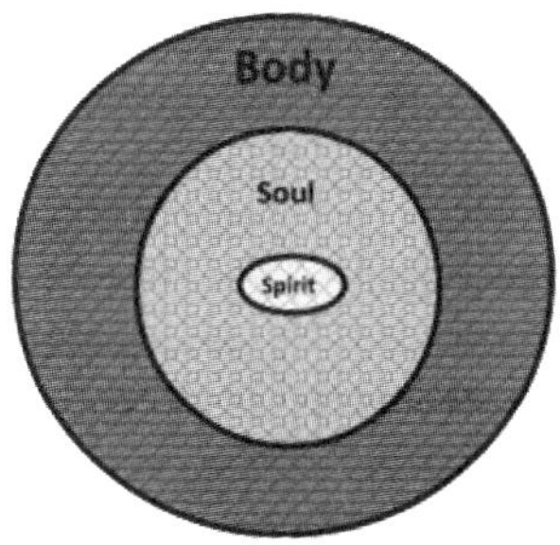


Unfortunately, many of us are like the above illustration. We have developed our physical body. Perhaps we even eat correctly, take vitamins daily and exercise regularly. Our body as well as our soul appears to be overwhelming our spirit which looks shriveled up.

Galatians 3:3 (Amplified) asks two vital questions in this situation. *"Are you so foolish and so senseless and so silly? Having begun [your new life spiritually] with the Holy Spirit, are you now reaching perfection [by dependence] on the flesh?"*

The answer to these questions is obvious.

We are not being led or controlled by the Holy Spirit. Instead, we are being dominated by the impulses of our physical body and the foolish excesses of our stubborn, unyielding soul.

Romans 8:5 (Amplified) provides us with God's perspective on this warfare between our spirit, soul and body. Listen carefully:

*"For those who are according to the flesh and controlled by its unholy desires, set their minds on and pursue those things which gratify the flesh. But those who are according to the Spirit and [controlled by the desires] of the Spirit, set their minds on and seek those things which gratify the (Holy) Spirit."*

If we make flawed decisions based upon our soulish nature such as being influenced by spicy TV ads aimed at soul and body, we are not being led by the Spirit. Of course, God's great desire for all mankind is that we would be led by His Spirit.

That's clearly the instruction of Galatians 5:16 (Amplified). *"...Walk and live [habitually] in the [Holy] Spirit [responsive to and controlled and guided by the Spirit; then you will certainly not gratify the cravings and desires of the flesh (of human nature without God)."*

Decisions based upon greed, pain, or covetousness (desiring something we do not have) are reflections of being dominated by the flesh.

Years ago I invested in an alternative energy project even though I had a "check" in my spirit about my decision. Within a brief period of time, I—and the other investors—realized the sad truth. All of our money had been stolen. In my case, I had a wrong motive and I failed to heed the Spirit's caution.

Often times, we fall into wrong choices because our spirit is undeveloped and shriveled up. We have never disciplined ourselves through regular study of God's Word, nor have we been willing to sit under the ministries of anointed men and women of God and learn to truly walk in the Spirit.

Hebrews 12:11 (Amplified) details the great benefit of God's discipline in the life of a believer.

*"For the time being no discipline brings joy, but seems grievous and painful; but afterwards it yields a peaceable fruit of righteousness to those who have been trained by it [a harvest of fruit which consists in righteousness—in conformity to God's will in purpose, thought and action, resulting in right living and right standing with God]."*

The above illustration looks considerably better. It reflects the Spirit of God becoming preeminent in a believer's life. As a result that person begins making decisions based upon what God's Word says and His specific counsel directs.

It means following the pattern of Romans 8:13 (Amplified): *"...through the power of the [Holy] Spirit you are [habitually] putting to death (making extinct, deadening) the [evil] deeds prompted by the body..."*

At times, the Spirit of God might whisper to us, "No, don't follow that path."

Our flesh would immediately cry out loudly: "Yes! Yes! Go for it! Do it! Do it! It's okay...everybody else is doing it."

If we're not careful, we listen to the louder voice and ignore the still, small voice. In some cases, we act "as though" we don't even hear God's voice.

When we have developed and fed our spirit, that trend gets reversed in our lives. We now hear the Spirit of God speaking *loudly*: "Don't do that!"

Our flesh has now become feeble and can only urge weakly: "It'll be okay. Go ahead and do it anyway."

We all still have to deal with the flesh and the soulish parts of our nature. But if we follow God's direction for our lives, the Spirit will be preeminent.

The result is something heavenly according to Romans 8:14 (Amplified): *"For all who are led by the Spirit of God are sons of God."*

Our last illustration reflects something the Lord spoke to me about one day. As I was thinking about the four previous illustrations, I heard Him say: "There's one more." I quickly replied "What is it?"

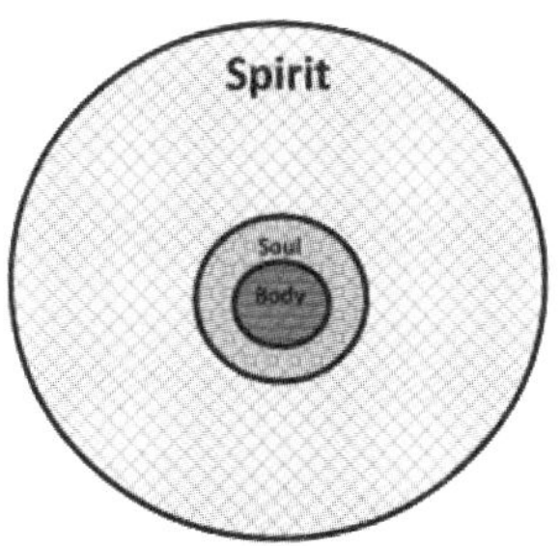


Immediately, I had a mental picture of this fifth illustration and the revelation came to me that this is what it means to be *"in the Spirit."*

It is a reflection of what God greatly desires in all of our lives. Our spirit is not confined to our body—that's how we can have out of body experiences. All of our spiritual senses are easily activated when we step into this arena.

Without question that was clearly in the heart of the apostle John when he penned these words in Revelation 1:10 (Amplified).

*"I was in the Spirit [rapt in His power] on the Lord's Day, and I heard behind me a great voice like the calling of a war trumpet."*

I believe your spirit can become larger than you are. In this dimension, you have come to the place where you clearly hear God's voice and you grasp what He is doing in the earth realm and your role in that unfolding plan for your life.

When I was newly married and fresh out of college,

my wife and I worked for a brief time with my father who owned a hardware and building supply business. He and I frequently clashed over how the company was operated. I thought I knew more than him because of my college degree in business.

Following a heated confrontation one afternoon, I quit and we moved to another state for ministry. After that move didn't work out, we relocated to California where I worked a secular job and helped with an outreach ministry.

During a lunch break one day, I heard the voice of the Lord speaking loudly to me. *"You need to return to Florida because your father needs you."*

I resisted those words at first but finally made the phone call. "What would you think of me coming back to work for you?" I asked when Dad answered. He replied: "I need you. How soon can you get here?"

It became a significant, life-changing moment for me. I humbled myself and went back to make things right with my Dad. If I hadn't obeyed the Holy Spirit with that phone call and the decision that followed, I probably wouldn't be in ministry today.

## Chapter 4

# Freedom from Idols

*"Therefore, having these promises, beloved, let us cleanse ourselves from all defilement of flesh and spirit, perfecting holiness in the fear of God."*

— 2 Corinthians 7:1 (NASB)

Are we *actually* supposed to cleanse ourselves from the deeds of the flesh?

I believe that's how we are intended to live as followers of Jesus. We are instructed to cleanse ourselves and quit looking at the lives of others, or focused on their misdeeds as an excuse for continuing in our own bad behavior.

You may remember that after his resurrection, Jesus appeared to the disciples and began giving them some instruction. Peter was specifically told: *"Follow Me!"* (John 21:19).

Turning around, Peter saw John standing nearby. *"Lord, and what about this man?"* he asked. Clearly, his focus was misplaced.

Jesus was quick to answer (John 21:22). *"If I want him to remain until I come, what is that to you? You follow Me!"*

Truthfully, it doesn't matter what anybody else does or doesn't do. Our calling is to follow the Lord.

So, we are to cleanse ourselves from all defilement of flesh and spirit. That's our challenge, and God has provided us with the spiritual means of completing that task.

Do you believe our spirit can be tainted by the things of the world? Clearly, 2 Corinthians 7:1 says to *"cleanse ourselves...of flesh and spirit."*

Some might suggest that the word for spirit actually means soul. Yet, the Greek word here is *pneuma*, and it is translated 375 times as spirit, three times as wind and two times as breath.

Obviously, our spirit can be terribly affected by a self-centered worldly pursuit. How can we cleanse ourselves from such defilement?

We can certainly pray and ask the Lord to remove this sin from our lives. He would probably respond with the plain-spoken instruction: *"Stop sinning."*

That's what Jesus did in dealing with the lame man healed at the pool of Bethesda, He said to him (John 5:14 Amplified), *"See, you are well! Stop sinning, or something worse may happen to you."*

Proverbs 1:10 (NASB) says *"My son, if sinners entice you, do not consent."*

Why are we asking God to do something He has already done? That sin was dealt with upon the cross of Jesus. The price for that sin was paid and victory was obtained. All we have to do now is accept what Jesus has already accomplished and *"stop sinning."*

I know a minister-friend who was struck down for about six weeks with a pinched nerve in his neck. The injury caused him to cancel a busy schedule of ministry and submit himself for regular treatment from a Christian osteopath.

My friend was in unrelenting pain day after day and terribly anxious about canceling weeks of ministry. Yet, one day while undergoing treatment, the osteopath spoke a word from heaven: "When you abuse or neglect your body, you deny God His rightful use of your life."

That minister-friend recognized the piercing truth of the doctor's words. He *had* abused his body through constant travel and meetings. He *had* neglected proper rest and care. He was actually denying God's rightful use of his life by simple disobedience involving his physical body.

Life-changing lessons ensued from that painful experience for my friend. He determined to pass those lessons on to help others.

Don't blame somebody else for your struggles. Each of us is responsible for every choice we make. Obviously, we are free to make whatever choice we want in life, but we are *not* free from the serious life-changing consequences of those choices.

## Forgiveness

How can believers act so petty, unloving and unforgiving with one another when Jesus has forgiven us of such gross sins and misdeeds?

Jesus acknowledges in Matthew 9:6 (NASB) that He had *"authority on earth to forgive sins"* Yet, we who claim to know and love Him, can act with such callous hearts and obstinate spirits in dealing with those who we believe have offended us.

Are we so blind that we cannot see that spirit of the Pharisee is within our heart and not the Spirit of the living God?

Without question, unforgiveness is the root cause of most friendships that break apart. It plays a significant role in many divorces. Husbands and wives alike refusing to simply say, "I have been wrong. Please forgive me."

Sadly, that same kind of unforgiveness often causes congregations to split asunder with people never dealing with their own culpability and wrong attitude.

## Holiness

Look at the next phrase in 2 Corinthians 7:1—*"perfecting holiness in the fear of the Lord."* Holiness can be a confounding subject for most believers. There are "holiness" churches in the Body of Christ, and the expression "holy" or "holiness" appears throughout Scripture.

Deuteronomy 7:6 says *"For you are a holy people to the Lord your God..."* That is clearly God's design for His people.

However, holiness is not following a list of do's and don'ts. It's simply becoming more like Jesus in every area of one's life. That possibility is very real based upon the last phrase of 1 John 4:17 which declares *"as He is, so also are we in this world."*

I've learned a great truth in my devotional life that we become more like the people we spend time with. That's one of the great benefits of intimacy with the Father. Unquestionably, we become more like the Lord because we spend time with Him.

So, holiness, which is a clear reflection of God's character and nature, is genuinely being who He has made us to be, which is naturally supernatural.

## Idols of the Heart

Ezekiel 14:1-5 speaks of a troubling time in Israel and

the very cause of that trouble: *"Then some elders of Israel came to me and sat down before me.*

*"And the word of the Lord came to me saying,*

*"Son of man, these men have set up their idols in their hearts and have put right before their faces the stumbling block of their iniquity. Shall I be consulted by them at all?*

*"Therefore speak to them and tell them, 'Thus says the Lord God, 'Any man of the house of Israel who sets up his idols in his heart, puts right before his face the stumbling block of his iniquity, and then comes to the prophet, I the Lord will be brought to give him an answer in the matter in view of the multitude of his idols."*

Now, get this important picture. These are elders of Israel—mature and seasoned priests—but God says they have a sinful problem. They're looking at their idols and won't listen to the Almighty. What could be worse for a priest of God?

Idols, such as the golden calf, were a common problem in Bible days. But most of us would be hard-pressed to identify idols in our day.

Let me help you with this list. Here are a few choice idols in people's lives: money, sports, jobs, cars, hobbies. Even, husbands, wives and children can be idols to certain people.

Idols have the dangerous potential of preventing us from receiving all that God has. They literally stop us from hearing the Word of the Lord in our lives.

An idol is anything that we place between ourselves

and God. 1 John 5:21 warns us to *"guard yourself from idols."*

We know that Romans 1:27 speaks of God "giving" people over to their lusts and desires of their flesh. All of these so-called lusts and desires were idols that had gained control of people's lives.

Psalm 115:4-8 gives us some revealing observations about idols:

*Their idols are silver and gold,*
*The work of man's hands.*
*They have mouths, but they cannot speak;*
*They have eyes, but they cannot see;*
*They have ears, but cannot hear;*
*They have noses, but they cannot smell;*
*They have hands, but they cannot feel;*
*They cannot make a sound with their throat.*
*Those who make them will become like them,*
*Everyone who trusts in them.*

When we trust in our idols, we become like them. Our spiritual senses of hearing, seeing, feeling are all blocked. When idols work on the inside, we become hardened to the influence of God's Spirit. It is impossible to become naturally supernatural when idols shape and influence our lives.

Without question, it is time to deal with these idols we have placed before our faces. The idols are keeping us from God's highest and best, and we are admonished to *"flee from idolatry"* (1 Corinthians 10:14).

Remember the words of Jonah 2:8 (NIV), *"Those who cling to worthless idols forfeit the grace that could be theirs."*

There is a price to pay to become naturally supernatural. But once you decide that's your goal, God will open the way for you to live the life He intended so that you can receive His freedom and liberty.

The decision is yours!

## Chapter 5

# The Transformed Life

*"Do not be conformed to this world...[fashioned after and adapted to its external, superficial customs], but be* *transformed* *by the [entire] renewal of your mind [by its new ideals and its new attitude]..."*

—Romans 12:2 (Amplified)

The word "transformed" here in Romans 12:2 is derived from the Greek word *metamorphoomai* from which comes the word "metamorphosis". According to *Webster's New Collegiate Dictionary*, metamorphosis means a "change of physical form, structure, or substance, especially by supernatural means."

Another definition from Webster's is "a marked and more or less abrupt change in the form or structure of an animal." In this sense, we are all familiar with the example of a caterpillar being transformed into a beautiful butterfly.

The same Greek word (*metamorphoomai)* is also used in Matthew 17:2 where Jesus was *"transfigured"* before Peter, James and John on the Mount of Transfiguration. In this usage, Jesus' face *"shone like the sun, and His garments became as white as light"* (NASB).

In Mark 9:2 the identical story is recorded that Jesus took these three disciples to the Mount and was *"transfigured"* before them. The Greek word *metamorphoomai* is also used in Mark's account.

Finally, *metamorphoomai* is also utilized in 2 Corinthians 3:18 in this manner: *"But we all, with unveiled face, beholding as in a mirror the glory of the Lord, are being transformed into the same image from glory to glory, just as from the Lord, the Spirit."*

It is quite evident from reading both Romans 12:2 and 2 Corinthians 3:18 that this transformation described is fully supernatural in every aspect.

On one hand, it brings vital revelation about the "born again" experience. And on the other hand, it also expresses God's holy desire for the life He intended each of His children to live—*transformed*—while upon this earthly journey.

How can a believer experience this great transformation? Is it a separate work of the Holy Spirit? Or, can I simply step into this spiritual dimension by an active pursuit of the Lord?

**Understanding Repentance**

Acts 3:19 (NASB) shows us the way to experience God's unfolding pathway to this magnificent life of great freedom and liberty in Christ.

*"Therefore repent and return, so that your sins may be wiped away, in order that times of refreshing may come from the Presence of the Lord."*

Years ago, I was in meetings where the mighty Presence of God came into the services, and people were being touched everywhere I looked. Actually, everybody appeared to be touched but me!

I was standing there wondering, "When is this ever going to get over with?" It was not a time of refreshing for me because I had not heeded the first part of that verse *"repent and return."*

What does the word "repent" mean?

Most people believe incorrectly that repent means to stop doing something negative and start doing something positive in one's life. Actually that's the *result* of repenting, but it's not what the word means.

"Repent" from the Greek is the word *metanoeo*, which literally means to change the way that you think. The Spirit Filled Life Bible says "repentance is a decision that results in a change of mind, which in turn leads to a change of purpose and action."

If we are going to experience God's supernatural, we must change the way we think about Him, about ourselves, about religious traditions, about the idols in our lives.

When we change the way we think about those things, our actions begin to change. The result brings us into developing our spirit and defeating the desires of the flesh. The same result is true when we change the way we think about sin in our lives or what it means to be filled with the Holy Spirit.

Without question, we have the ability to set our mind on whatever we desire. However, we must also recognize the consequences of that ability. Listen to Romans 8:6, *"For the mind set on the flesh is death, but the mind set on the Spirit is life and peace..."*

What would happen today if you consciously set your mind upon the Spirit of God?

If your mind is focused upon worldly pursuits, the result is death. It's like a literal dead-end street, but the mind set on the spirit produces two important results—life and peace. The two things we all long for—life and peace—become ours.

## The Control Center of our Lives

The mind is the control center of our lives. That's where the battle happens every day, and each of us chooses which direction we will follow—either the spirit (and God's will and purpose), or the flesh (the evil one's plan).

Did you know the brain is simply a physical organ of your body?

Of course the word "brain" never appears in the Bible. The brain only responds to the thoughts in our minds. It functions much like a computer. It has a hard drive and stores all kinds of information. But our body responds to the thoughts of the mind.

I recently conducted an unrehearsed experiment during a weekend seminar in Moravian Falls. I had my audience stand and I instructed everyone to "think about the most *horrible* event in your life."

Almost immediately, I noticed that faces had frowns and harsh looks. A few had the look of agony on their face. Shallow breathing was obvious with some. Heads dropped and shoulders sagged.

Then, I announced: "I want everyone to think of the *best* event in your life—the time God came through on your behalf and turned your upsetting night into a sunshine-filled day!"

Immediately, heads came up. Shoulders went back. People began to breathe deeply. Smiles lit up happy faces. Some raised their hands to the Lord acknowledging what He had done on their behalf.

What was the difference? People's bodies were responding

to the thoughts of their minds—and that is precisely what each of us does daily!

## Changing the Way We Think

Dr. Caroline Leaf (who has spoken at one of our North Carolina conferences) has authored some amazing books such as *Who Switched Off My Brain?* and *Switch on Your Brain*. However, the focus of her books is more about the mind than the brain.

She says that 87 to 95 percent of all illness is a direct result of a person's thought life. By itself, fear triggers more than 1400 physical and chemical responses and activates some 30 different hormones.

If we are going to become naturally supernatural, we must change the way that we think. Romans 12:2 (NASB) offers great advice in that struggle. *"And do not be conformed to this world, but be transformed by the renewing of your mind, so that you may prove, what the will of God is, that which is good and acceptable and perfect."*

If your mind is not renewed, transformation becomes very difficult in a believer's life. That word *"renewed"* means to make new. It literally means to renovate.

What happens when a building gets renovated? All the old stuff gets torn out and brand new stuff is installed. If you snap a before-and-after photo, it doesn't even look like the same place.

It's absolutely vital that we renovate our mind. We

must destroy every thought that comes into our head which resists the knowledge of God.

The process is two-fold. We must tear out the old thought patterns, and the other half is replacing it with all new thoughts. Remember the words of 1 Corinthians 2:16, *"...But we have the mind of Christ."*

We can choose to have the mind of Christ operative in our lives. In every circumstance stop and think, "What would Jesus do right now?" We can absolutely renovate our mind and that brings trans-formation into our lives.

Colossians 3:2 (NASB) tells us, *"Set your mind on the things above, not on things that are on earth."* It's very difficult to become spiritually-minded when you are thinking worldly thoughts.

Listen to the healing prescription of Philippians 4:6 in dealing with problems, *"Be anxious for nothing, but in everything by prayer and supplication with thanksgiving let your requests be made known to God."*

That's fairly simple. We are to worry about nothing, and pray about everything!

Just a few days ago I heard a minister-friend talking about how "worried" he was about some situation with a family member. I sought to encourage him but he persisted with worry.

Philippians 4:7 says *"And the peace of God, which surpasses all comprehension, will guard your hearts and your minds in Christ Jesus."*

Can you imagine this incredible possibility—experiencing "the peace of God" in your heart and mind—at the same time? The result is no more anxiety and no more fear, and having the peace of God continuously ruling and reigning in your life.

Philippians 4:8, *"Finally, brethren, whatever is true, whatever is honorable, whatever is right, whatever is pure, whatever is lovely, whatever is of good repute, if there is any excellence and if anything worthy of praise, dwell on these things."*

Verse eight tells us the way we are supposed to think all day long. Are you thinking like that? Or, are you full of anxiety?

Philippians 4:9 declares *"The things you have learned and received and heard and seen in me, practice these things, and the God of peace will be with you."*

Do you know the meaning of the word "practice"? It means repeating something over and over, and over *again* until you get it right.

There's a lot of trial and error with practice. You make a lot of mistakes in practicing. I learned that in college when I participated in track events by throwing the javelin. But you can't give up and you can't stop because of disappointment or failure.

Hebrews 5:14 (NASB) calls to mind the further value of this discipline of practice. *"But solid food is for the mature, who because of practice have their senses trained to discern good and evil."*

You have to determine you're going to change the way you think about yourself, about God, about religious tradition, and about the fleshly desires that seemingly assault your mind.

It is in the midst of such encounters in pursuit of God that we lay aside our old life and *"old self"* that is constantly *"being corrupted"* with *"lusts of deceit"* (Ephesians 4:22).

Accordingly, God brings a great renewal into our lives, and we are *"renewed in the spirit of our mind"* and we *"put on the new self, which is created in the likeness of God"* (Ephesians 4:23-24).

The spirit is the key place where the born again experience genuinely happens, but we begin to reflect the God-centered life in the way we think.

## The Power of the Tongue

Ephesians 4:22-24 (Amplified) makes a powerful statement about our words:

*"Let no foul or polluting language, nor evil word, nor unwholesome or worthless talk [ever] come out of your mouth, but only such [speech] as is good and beneficial to the spiritual progress of others, as is fitting to the need and the occasion, that it may be a blessing and give grace (God's favor) to those who hear it."*

Did you know that whatever is often on our mind has a terrible way of coming out of our mouth at some point? I *know* that experience first-hand.

If there is an area of the old life that troubles new believers more than any other, it is probably grappling with the power of the tongue. But it's not just the newcomers to the faith, it's also some of the old-timers who have a problem with their tongue.

Proverbs 30:32 (Amplified) gives us this piece of priceless advice. *"If you have...thought evil, lay your hand upon your mouth."* Don't say it!

Why should we put a hand over our mouth?

Proverbs 18:21 (Amplified) confirms the terrible danger in our words. *"Death and life are in the power of the tongue, and they who indulge in it shall eat the fruit of it [for death or life]."*

For instance, I have discovered that faith-inspired words are power containers and possess the capacity to change the atmosphere anywhere we speak them. Words can bring life or death. Most of us have truly never understood the power of our words.

For instance, have you ever observed how encouraging words to a downcast person changes their outlook on life?

The exact opposite is true with negative words. They have an equally destructive way of wounding or hurting others, or, making a bad situation worse!

The psalmist knew something about the value of the proper use of the tongue. Psalm 39:1 (NASB) says *"I will guard my ways that I may not sin with my tongue; I will guard my mouth as with a muzzle..."*

Did you know that the average person has somewhere between 30,000 to 60,000 thoughts in a single day?

Without question, what people say is a direct byproduct of their thought life. That's why we need to be careful about the words that we speak and the thoughts that we think.

In Psalm 19:14 (NASB) David presents a heartfelt cry to God about his words and thoughts. *"Let the words of my mouth and the meditation of my heart be acceptable in Your sight, O Lord, my rock and my Redeemer."*

Nothing is truly more reflective of a believer's transformed life than the way they think and the way they speak.

## Chapter 6

# Prayer of Activation

*"...Believing-prayer will heal you, and Jesus will put you on your feet. And if you've sinned, you'll be forgiven—healed inside and out...The prayer of a person living right with God is something powerful to be reckoned with..."*

— James 5:15-16 (The Message)

*[As you pray this prayer of activation, expect that God will respond to your petitions, believe for answers and position yourself to receive from heaven.]*

Father, I thank You for Your Word on the life You intended for me to live, and the great significance that Your purpose has for my life.

God, I pray for a release of wisdom and understanding right now for the life you intended for me to live and an everyday awareness of Your Spirit leading and guiding me into supernatural realms.

Lord, I will embrace with my whole heart this God-intended purpose for my life. In the same way, I will consciously reject the distractions that have kept me from Your highest and best.

Father, I pray for a great supernatural release of Your holy power into my life enabling me to daily walk by the Spirit, subdue my fleshly nature, and manifest the genuine fruit of the Holy Spirit.

God, I thank You that You will guide my very steps as I seek to "fully" obey Your direction and that You will show, reveal and manifest Yourself to me.

Lord, I pray for a yielded heart as You separate me from profane things and bring me forth as a pure and wholly consecrated vessel to You.

Father, I thank You for great freedom from idols of the heart, and that I walk in heartfelt forgiveness and true holiness in every dimension of my life.

God, I pray for a continual transformation of the Holy Spirit in me that is reflected by an attitude of repentance, right thoughts and a subdued tongue.

In the Name of Jesus, I completely yield myself to You for an on-going work of the renewing of my mind that I might become naturally supernatural.

# Prayer of Salvation

The most important decision anyone can make in life is to receive Jesus Christ as Lord and Savior. You can make that life-changing decision right now by simply praying the following prayer out loud with me:

**Lord Jesus, I ask You to forgive me of my sins and to cleanse me from those things that have kept me in bondage. I surrender to you today. I ask You to come into my heart and be my Lord and Savior.**

**I believe that You are the Son of God and that You were raised from the dead. Thank You, for hearing my prayer and giving me a new life as a child of God.**

**In Your holy Name, I pray, Amen.**

*[If you prayed that simple prayer with me, why don't you take a few minutes and write me about your decision for Jesus.]*

## About the Co-author...

**ROBERT PAUL LAMB** has preached the Gospel in some seventeen nations of the earth. However, he is best known for writing over 47 books (with over four million in print), many of which were written on the lives of exceptional men and women of God. He is the co-author of the book, *Open My Eyes, Lord.*

For book, CD, or MP3 orders,
please contact:

**Open Heaven Publications**
*an outreach of Gary Oates Ministries, Inc.*
P.O. Box 457/Moravian Falls, 28654 USA
336-667-2333
info@GaryOates.com

For more information, visit our website:

www.GaryOates.com